THE PHILLIP KEVEREN SERIES   PIANO SOLO

FIDDLIN' AT THE PIANO

— PIANO LEVEL —
LATE INTERMEDIATE/EARLY ADVANCED

ISBN 978-1-4584-9125-1

HAL•LEONARD®
CORPORATION

7777 W. BLUEMOUND RD. P.O. BOX 13819 MILWAUKEE, WI 53213

In Australia Contact:
Hal Leonard Australia Pty. Ltd.
4 Lentara Court
Cheltenham, Victoria, 3192 Australia
Email: ausadmin@halleonard.com.au

Visit Hal Leonard Online at
www.halleonard.com

Visit Phillip at
www.phillipkeveren.com

T0056511

PREFACE

I have wonderful memories of fiddle music from my youth. My parents loved to attend the National Oldtime Fiddlers' Contest in Weiser, Idaho. The musicianship was breathtaking – truly virtuosic. Although I was studying classical piano, a completely different pursuit, the event really inspired my musical development.

Many years later I rediscovered this tradition in the bluegrass players I have encountered here in Nashville, Tennessee. I have enjoyed many nights of superb music making at the The Station Inn and other venues in "Music City."

This collection features 22 classics from the world of fiddle music made accessible for the solo pianist. I hope you enjoy fiddlin' at the piano!

Sincerely,

Phillip Keveren

BIOGRAPHY

Phillip Keveren, a multi-talented keyboard artist and composer, has composed original works in a variety of genres from piano solo to symphonic orchestra. Mr. Keveren gives frequent concerts and workshops for teachers and their students in the United States, Canada, Europe, and Asia. Mr. Keveren holds a B.M. in composition from California State University Northridge and a M.M. in composition from the University of Southern California.

BILL CHEATHAM

Traditional
Arranged by Phillip Keveren

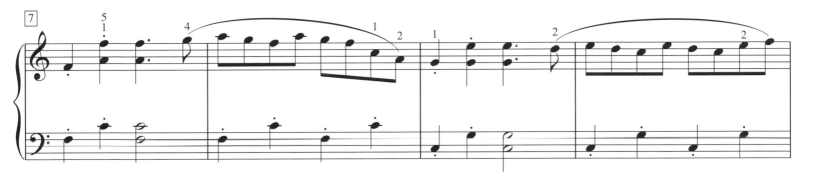

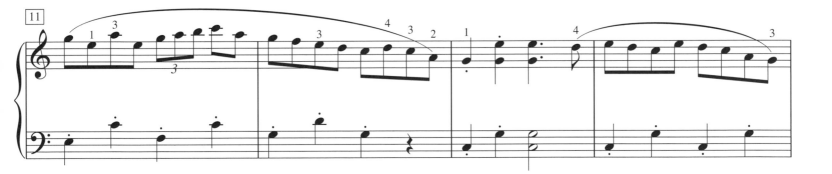

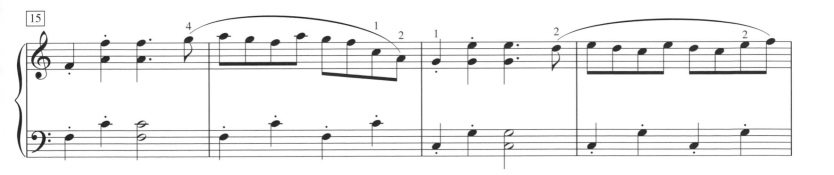

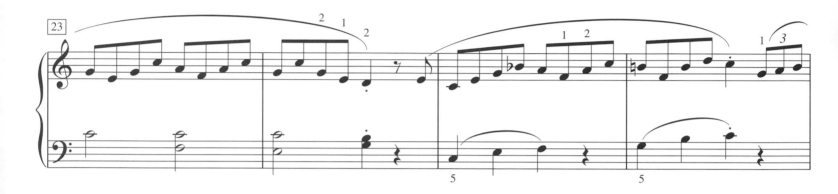

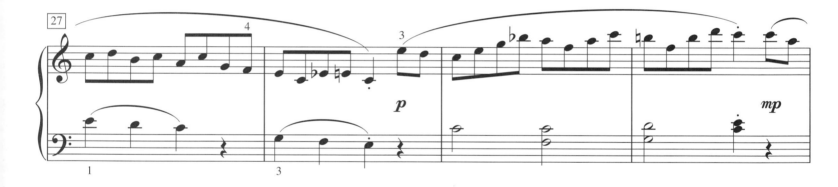

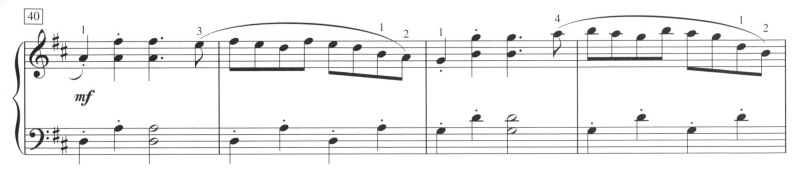
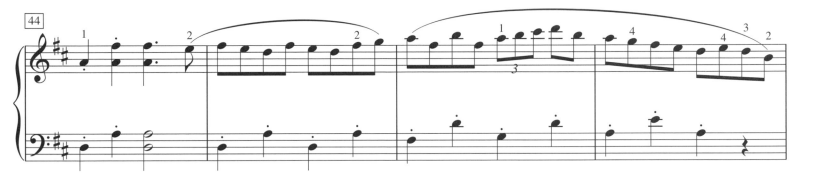
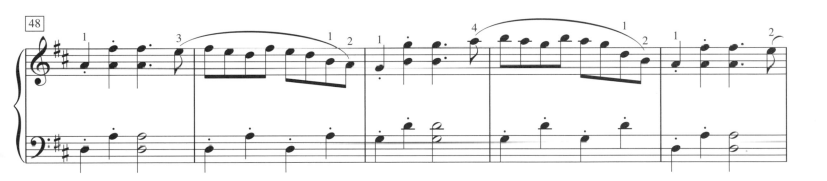
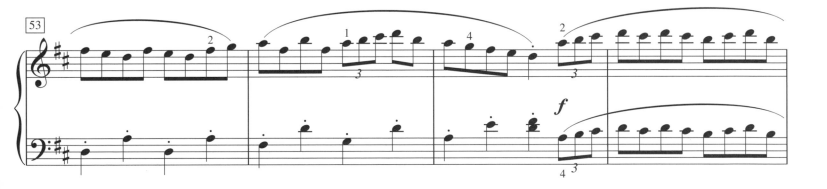
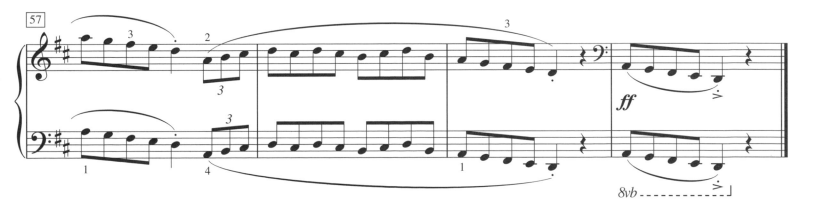

THE BLACKEST CROW

Traditional
Arranged by Phillip Keveren

Lament; with freedom (♩ = 92–96)

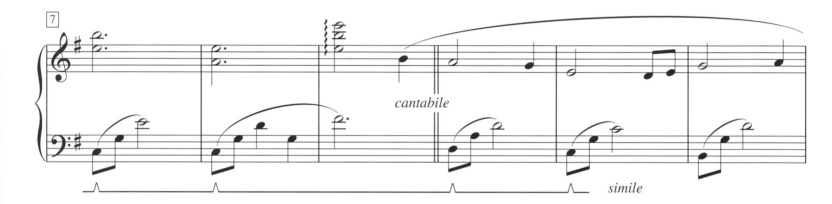

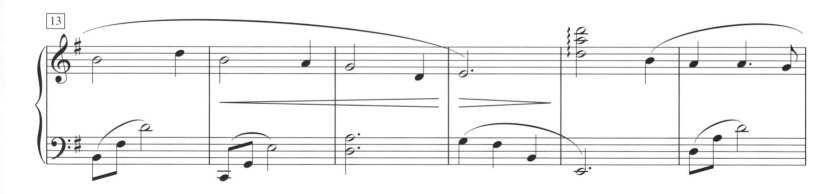

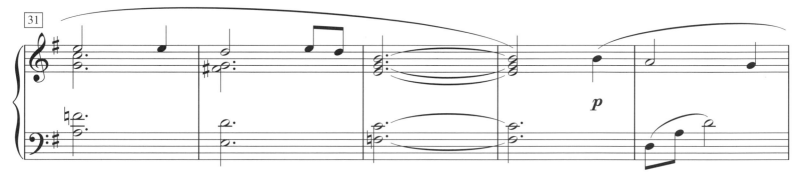

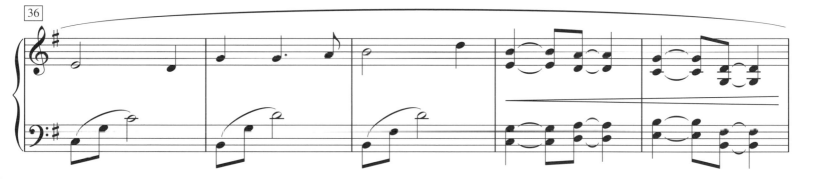

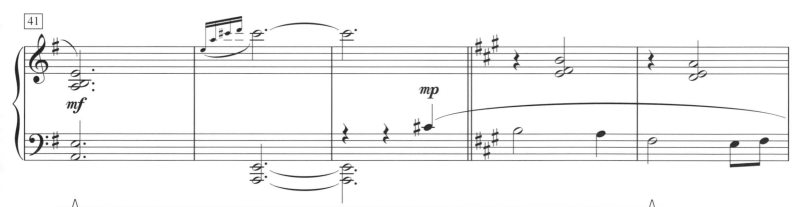

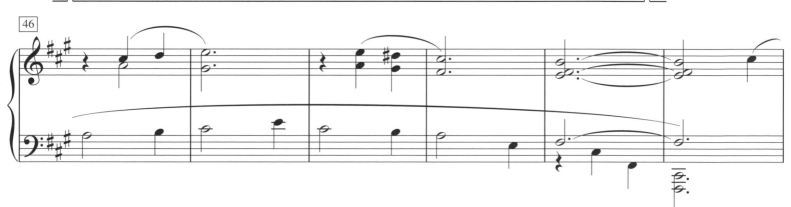

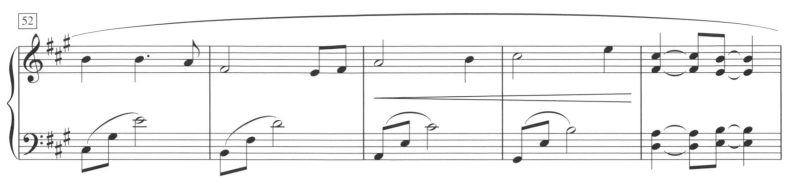

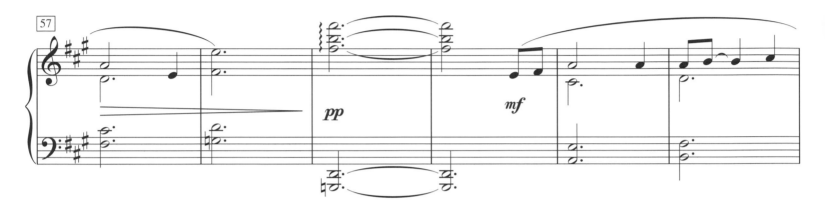

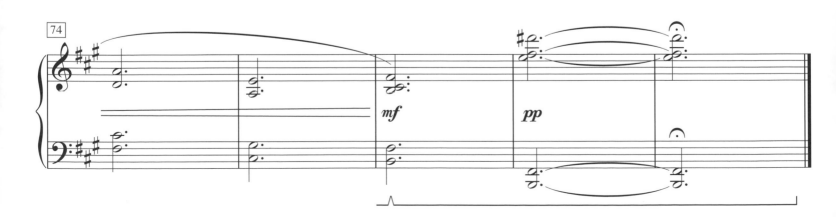

DOWN IN THE WILLOW GARDEN

Traditional
Arranged by Phillip Keveren

Poignantly (♩ = 100)

With pedal

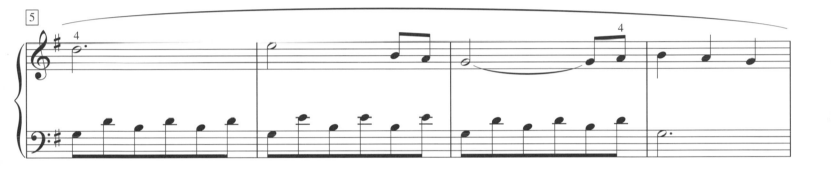

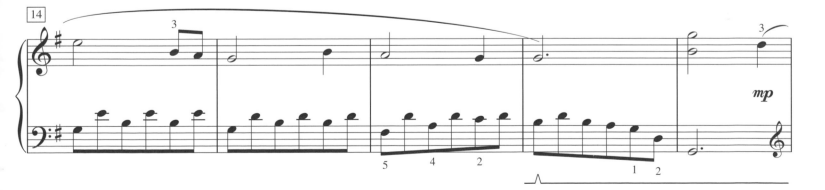

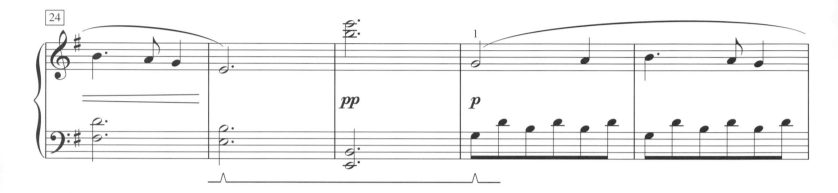

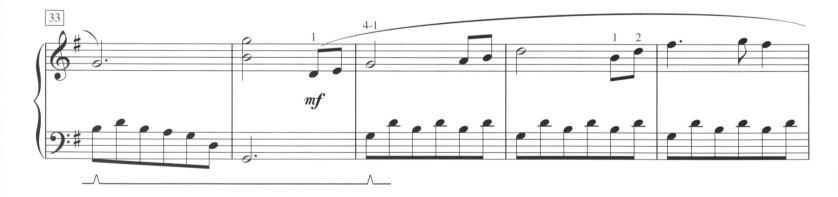

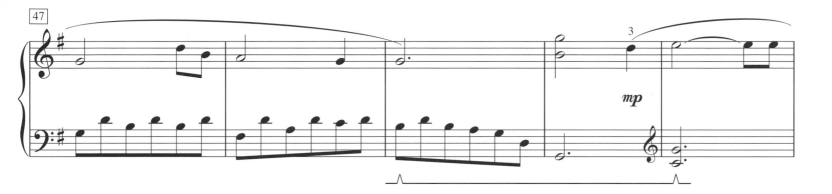

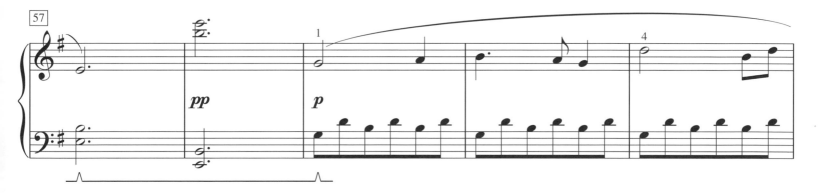

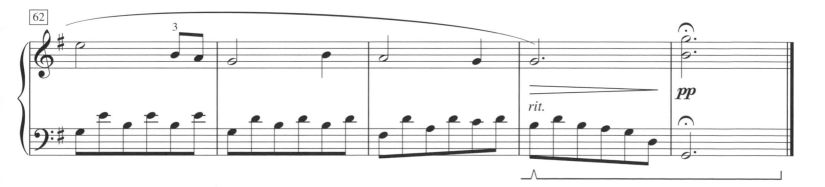

DOWN TO THE RIVER TO PRAY

Traditional
Arranged by Phillip Keveren

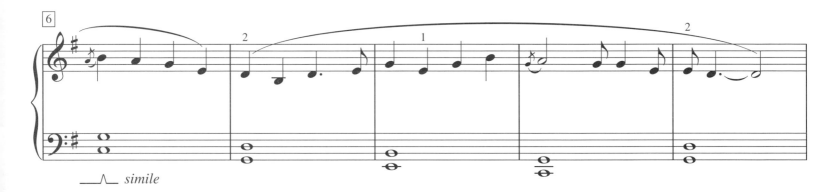

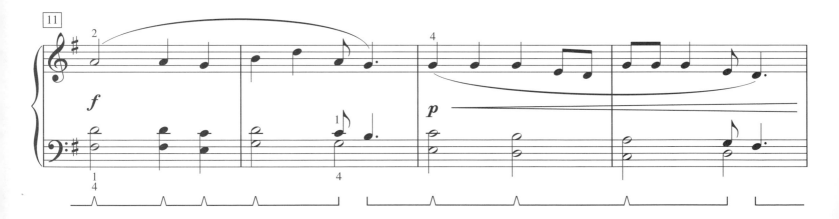

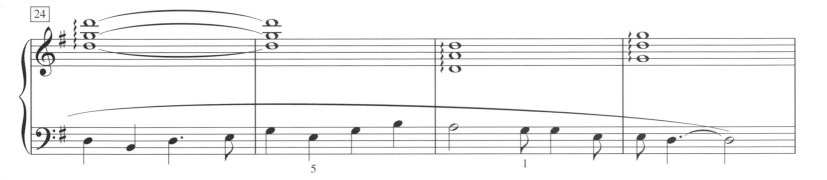

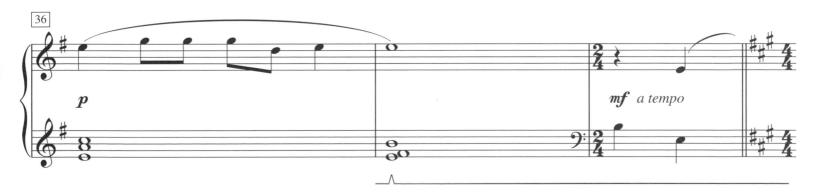

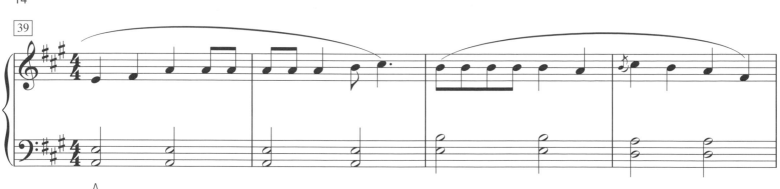

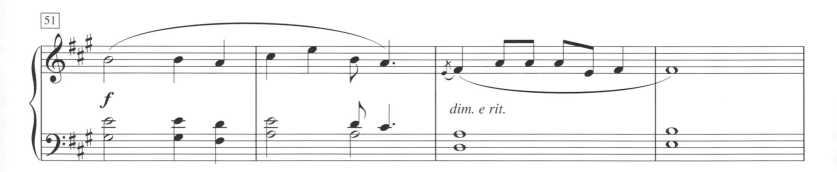

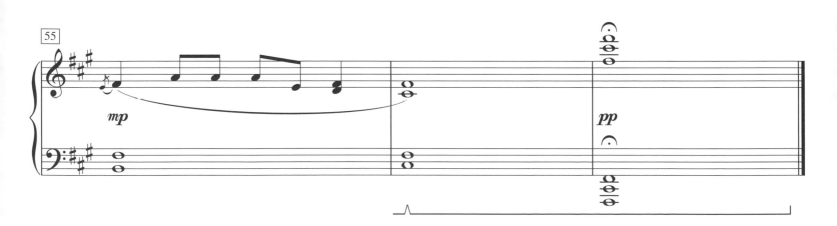

GREAT SPECKLED BIRD

Traditional Gospel Hymn
Arranged by Phillip Keveren

Medium Swing (♩ = 116)

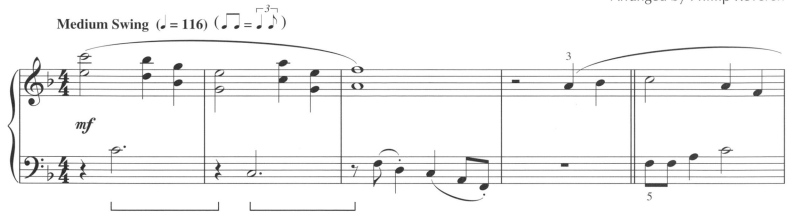

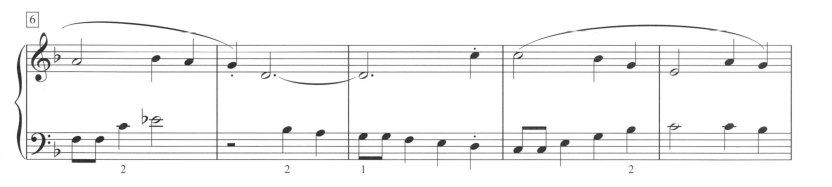

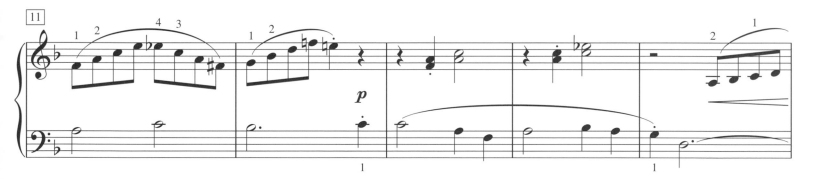

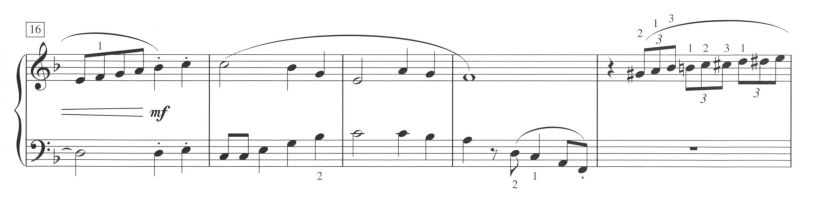

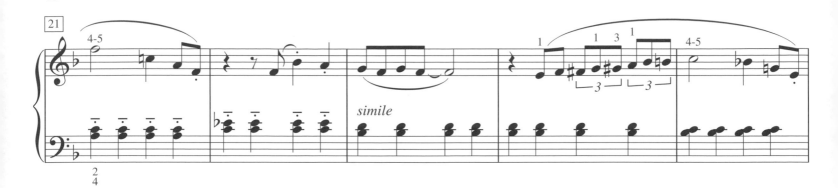

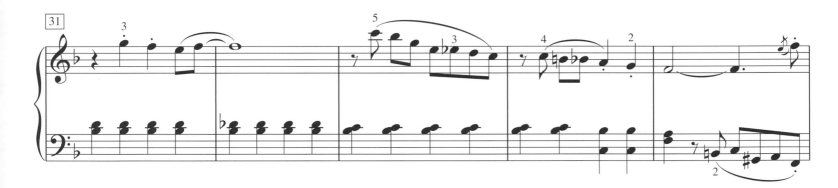

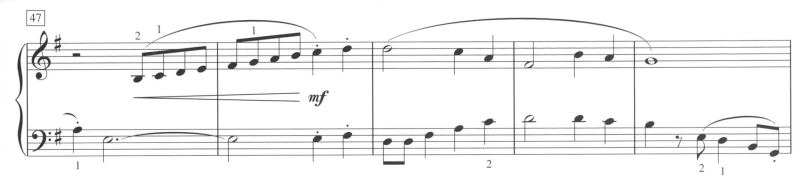

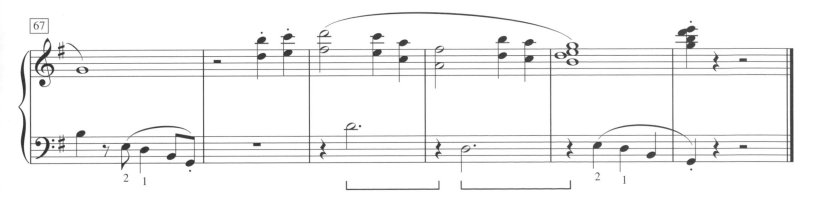

EIGHTH OF JANUARY

Traditional
Arranged by Phillip Keveren

Pluggin' Along (♩ = 80)

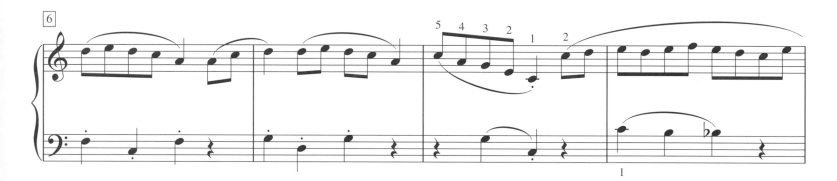

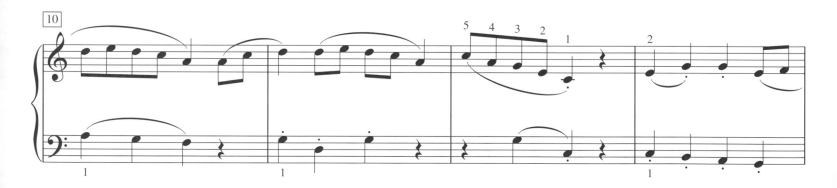

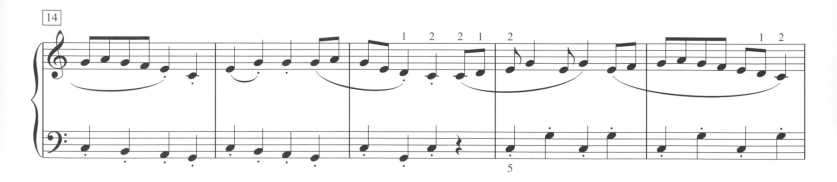

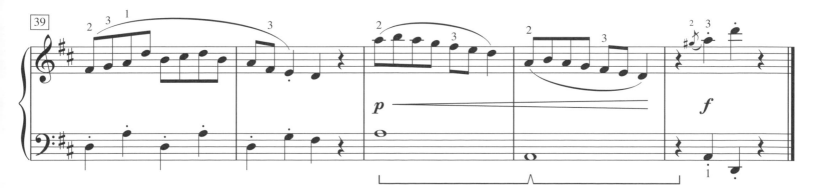

HORNPIPE MEDLEY

Arranged by Phillip Keveren

"College Hornpipe" (Traditional)

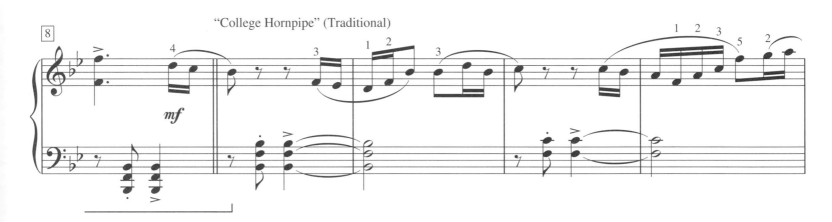

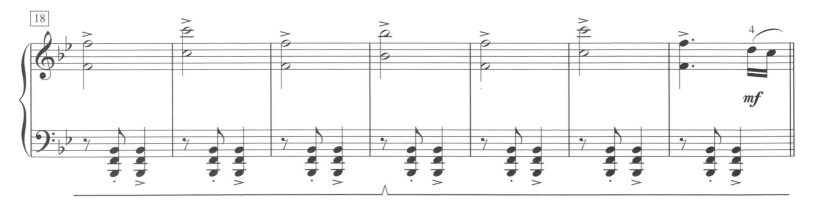

"Niagara Hornpipe" (Traditional)

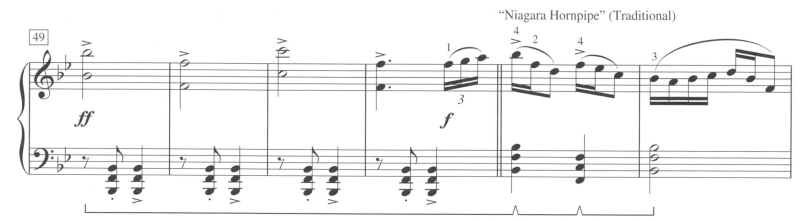

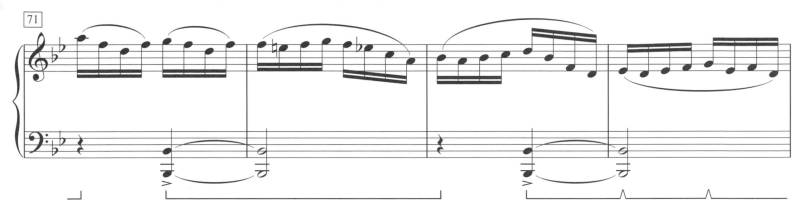

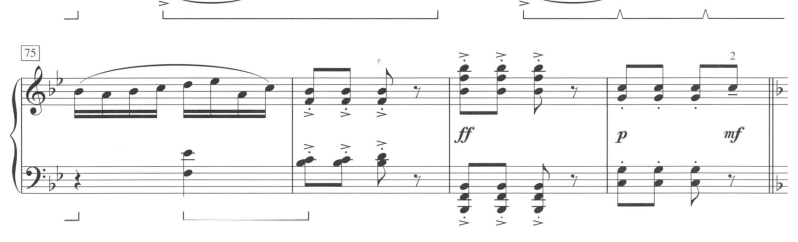

"Fisher's Hornpipe" (Traditional)

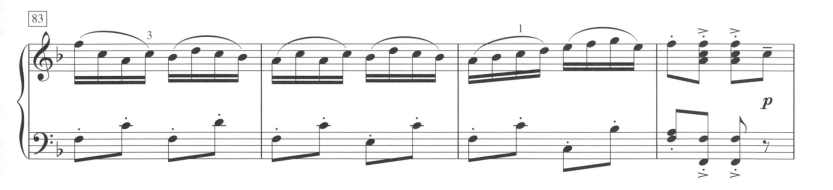

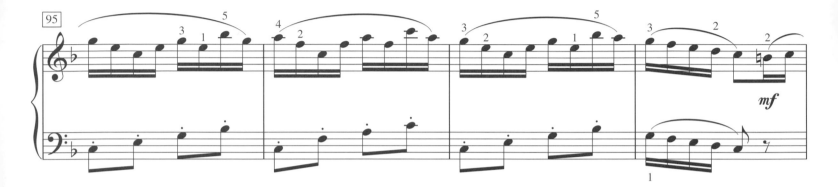

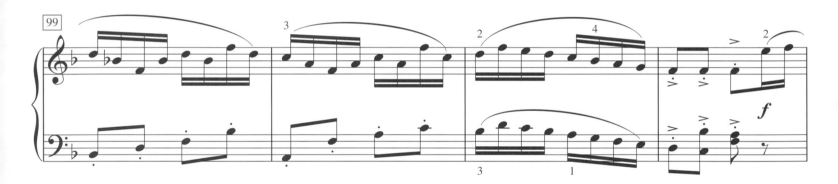

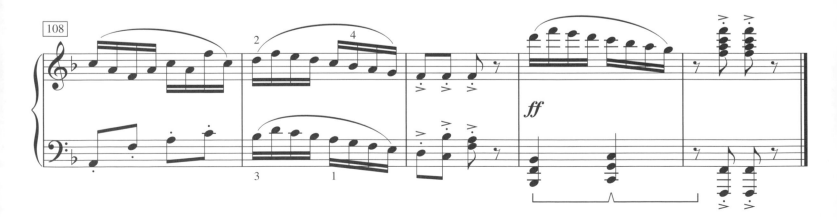

THE IRISH WASHERWOMAN

Irish Folksong
Arranged by Phillip Keveren

26

"Teetotal Jig" (Traditional)

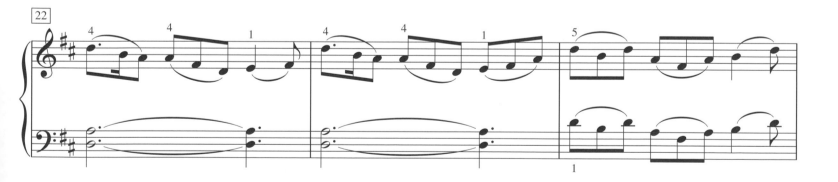

32

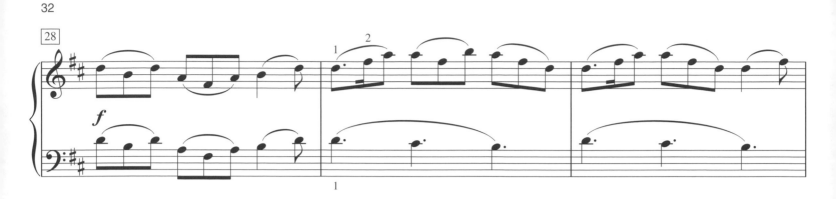

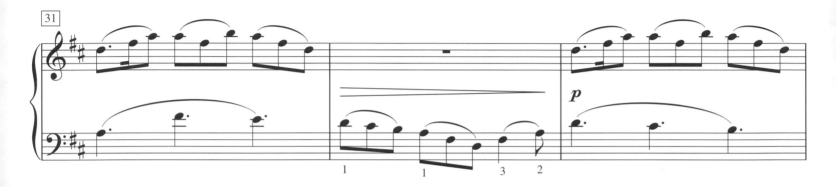

"Whiskey and Beer Jig" (Traditional)

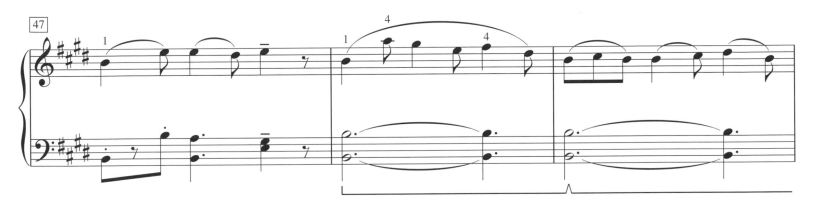

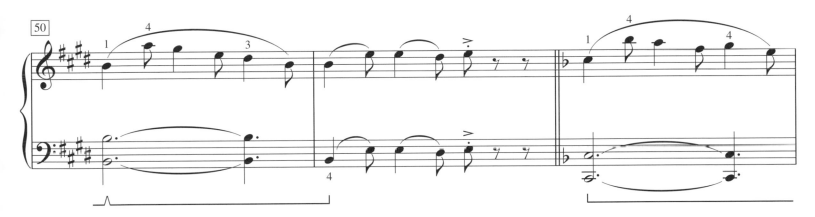

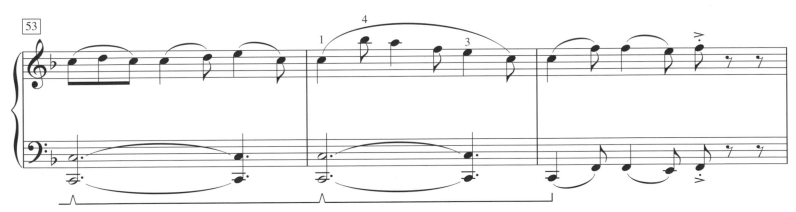

"Andrew Carey's Jig" (reprise)

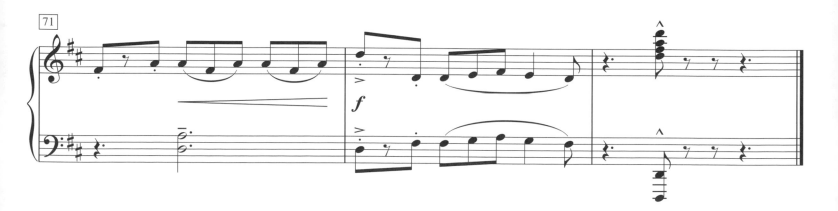

MISS McCLEOD'S REEL

Traditional
Arranged by Phillip Keveren

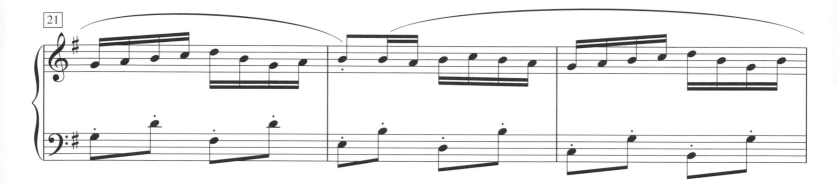

LITTLE DRUMMER'S JIG

Traditional
Arranged by Phillip Keveren

OH, THEM GOLDEN SLIPPERS

Words and Music by
JAMES A. BLAND
Arranged by Phillip Keveren

Kickin' (♩ = 120)

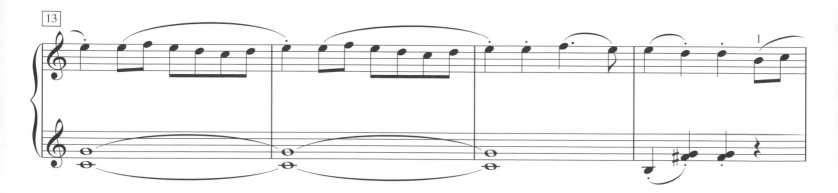

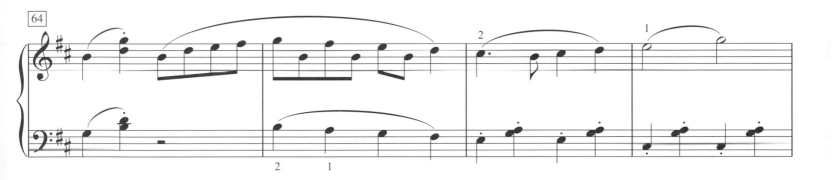

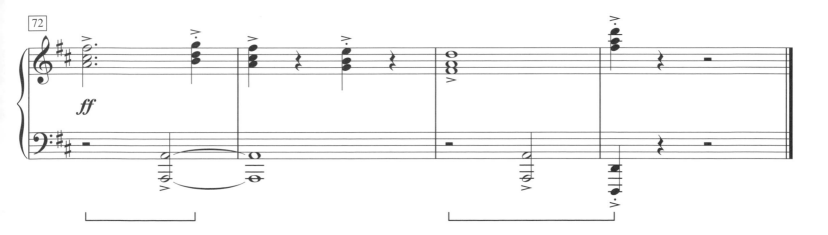

OVER THE WATERFALL

Traditional
Arranged by Phillip Keveren

RED WING

Words by THURLAND CHATTAWAY
Music by KERRY MILLS
Arranged by Phillip Keveren

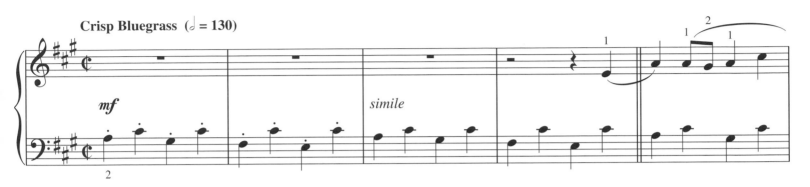

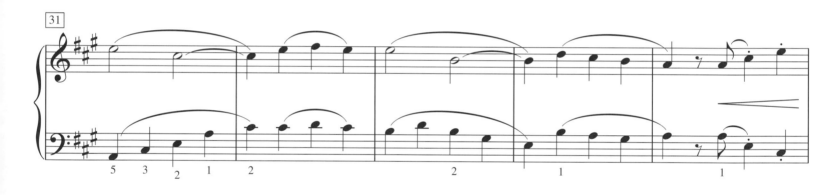

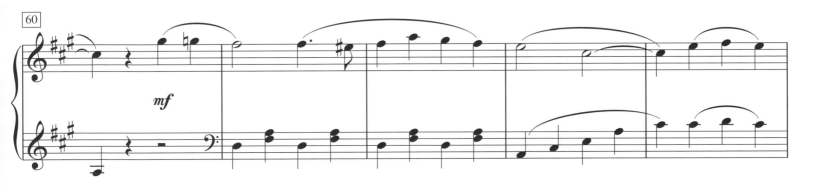

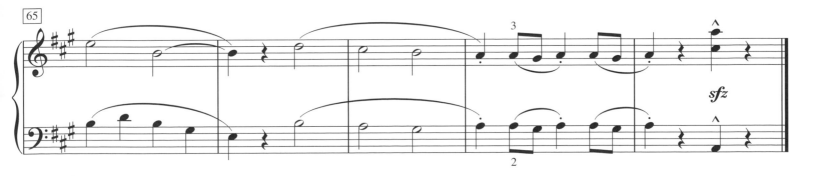

REILLY'S REEL

Traditional
Arranged by Phillip Keveren

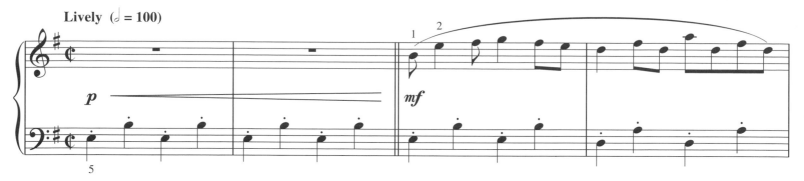

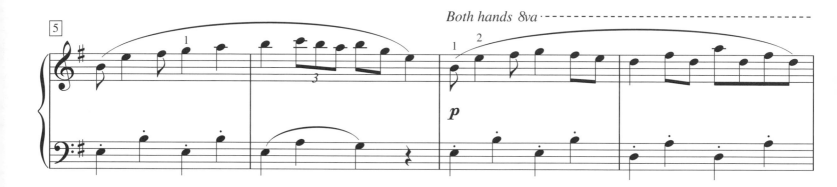

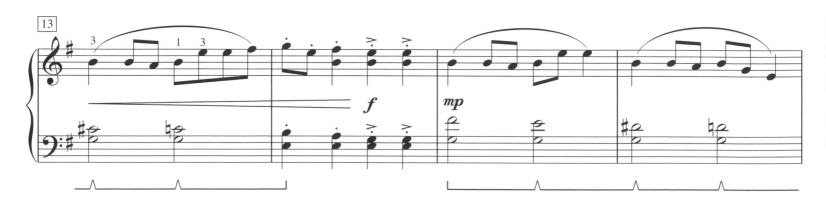

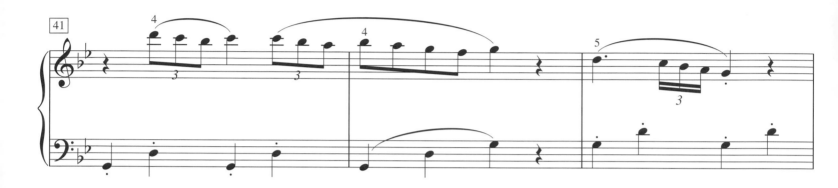

RUSTIC DANCE

Traditional
Arranged by Phillip Keveren

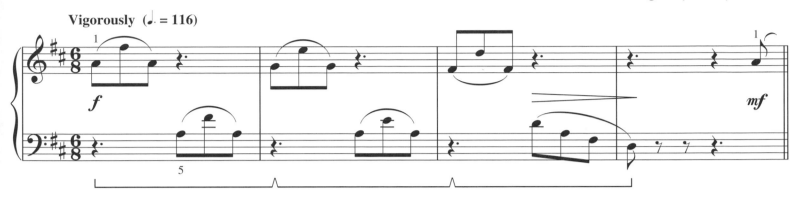

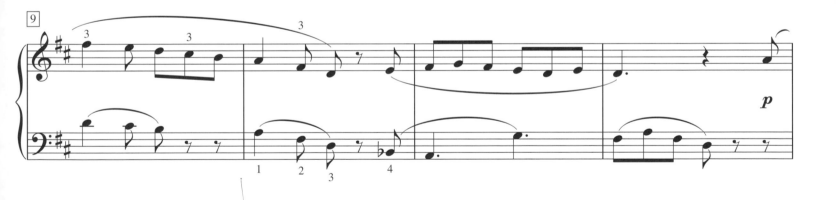

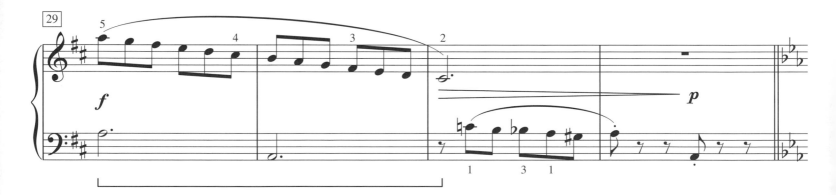

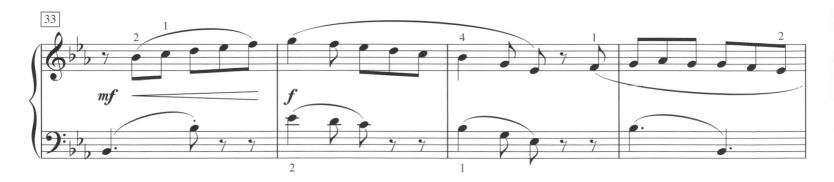

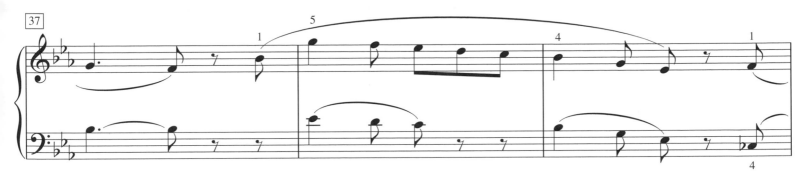

ROLL IN MY SWEET BABY'S ARMS

Traditional
Arranged by Phillip Keveren

Lickety-split (♩ = 144)

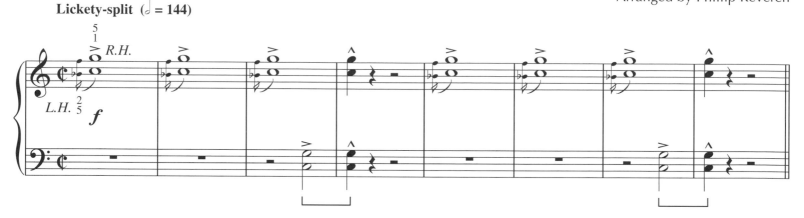

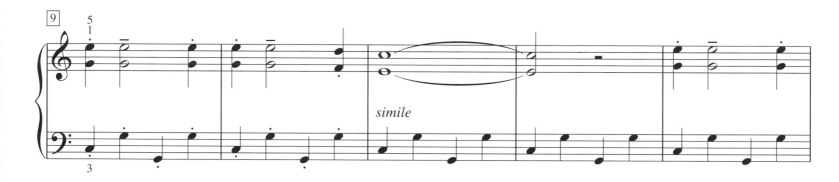

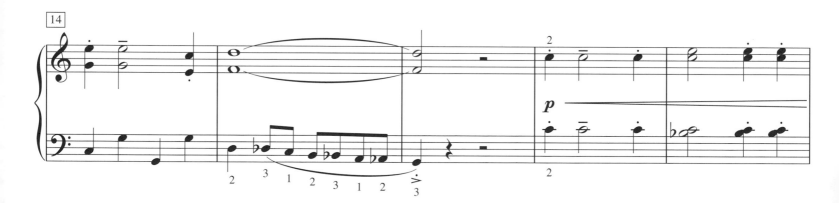

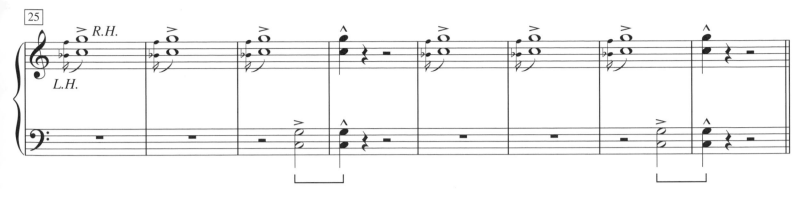

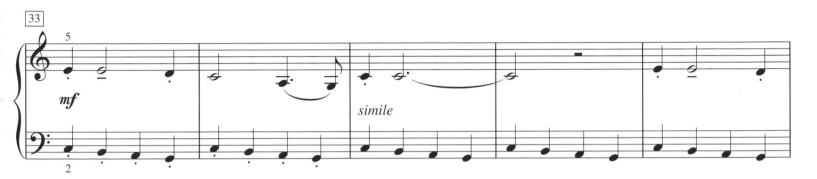

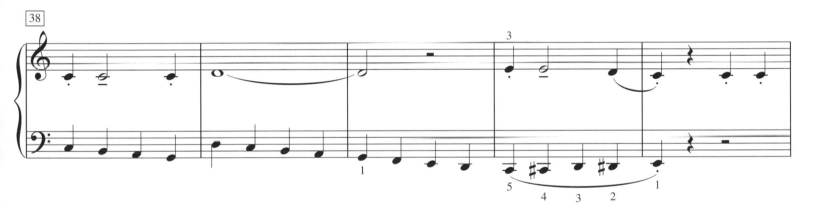

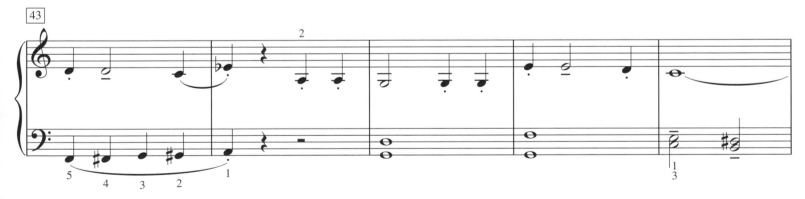

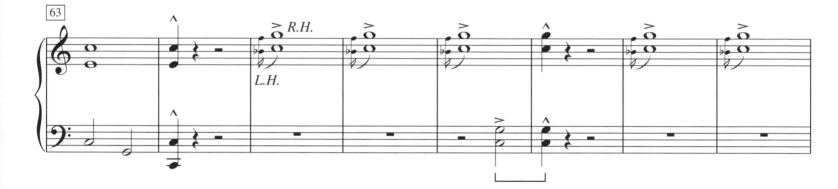

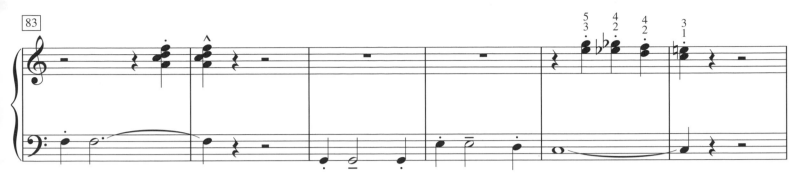

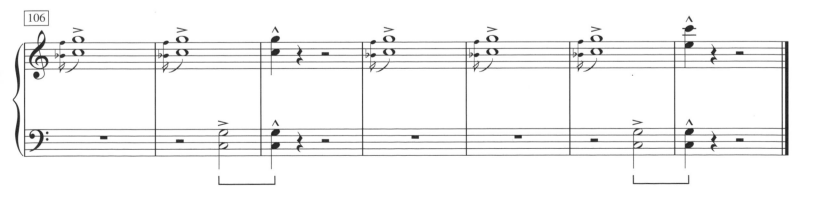

TURKEY IN THE STRAW

American Folksong
Arranged by Phillip Keveren

Bright Hoedown ($\quad$ = 116)

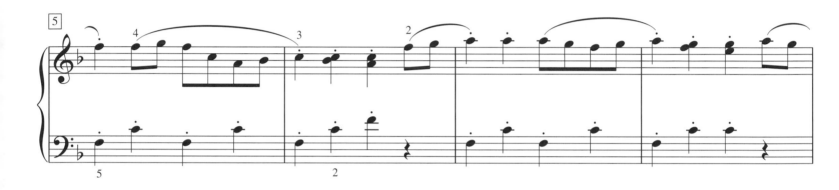

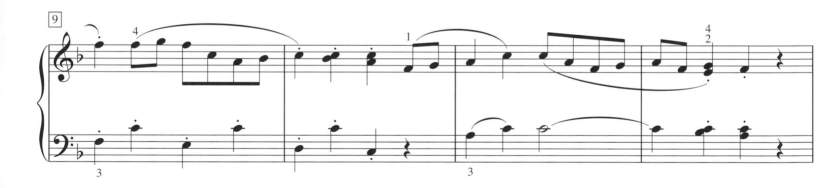

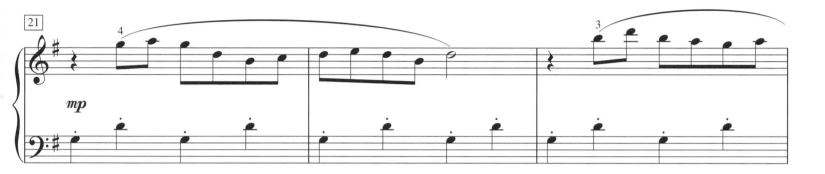

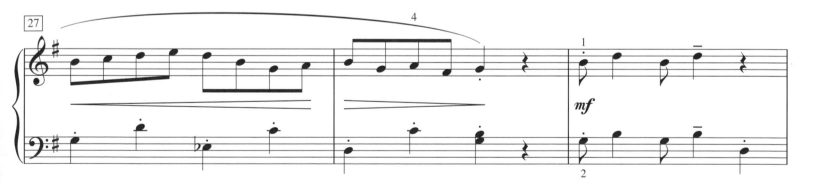

64

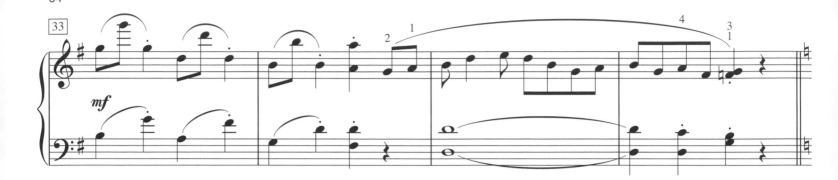

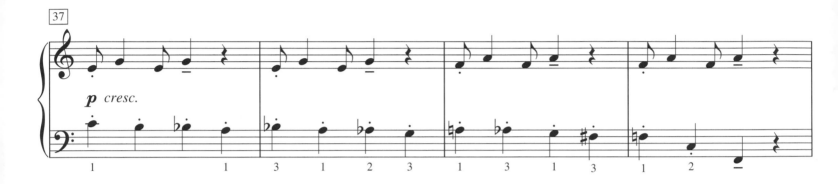

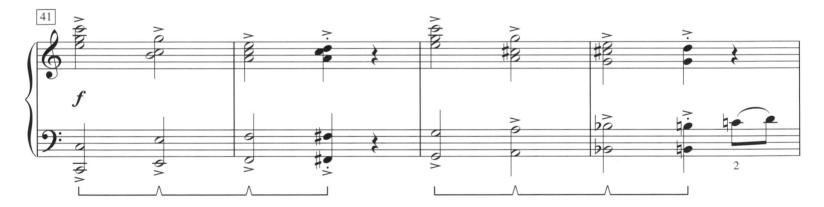

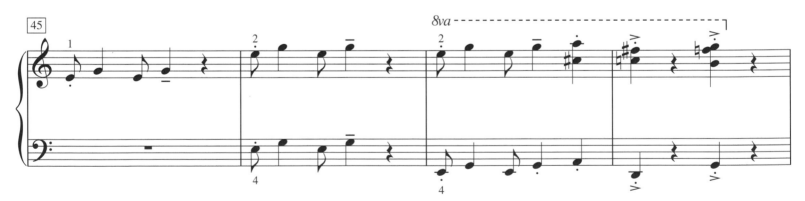

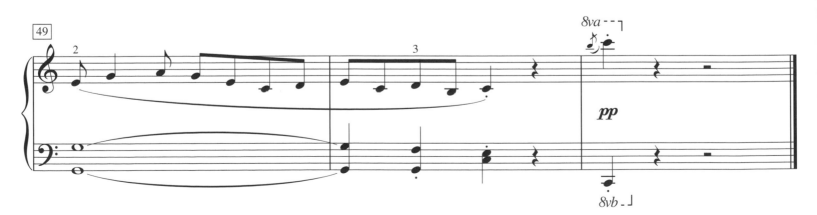